You KNOW You're 40 When...

Also by ANN HODGMAN

My Babysitter Is a Vampire (children's series)
Beat This! Cookbook
Beat That! Cookbook
One Bite Won't Kill You
1,003 Great Things About . . . series (coauthor)
I Saw Mommy Kicking Santa Claus

BROADWAY BOOKS

New York

You KNOW You're  40 When...

ANN HODGMAN
and
PATRICIA MARX

Illustrated by TAYLOR LEE

A John Boswell Associates Book

BROADWAY

Broadway Books titles may be purchased for business or promotional use or for
special sales. For information, please write to Special Markets Department,
Random House, Inc., 1745 Broadway, New York, NY 10019.

PRINTED IN THE UNITED STATES OF AMERICA

BROADWAY BOOKS and its logo, a letter B bisected on the diagonal, are trade-
marks of Random House, Inc.

Visit our website at www.broadwaybooks.com

First edition published 2004

Book design by Judith Stagnitto Abbate
Illustrated by Taylor Lee

Library of Congress Cataloging-in-Publication Data
Hodgman, Ann.
You know you're 40 when— / Ann Hodgman and Patricia Marx.—1st ed.
p.   cm.
1. Aging—Humor.   I. Title: You know you're forty when . . . .
II. Marx, Patricia (Patricia A.)   III. Title.
PN6231.A43H63 2005
818'.5402—dc22
2004045867

ISBN 0-7679-1739-1

10

Introduction

TURNING FORTY may not be much fun—but it sure is funny.

When did your *real* body get switched with this flabby, middle-aged one? Who tinkered with your metabolism behind your back? Where's the rock star you were going to be? And where did your motorcycle go? How did you end up with a minivan?

We can remember when our parents turned forty; they seemed ancient, if not middle-aged. (Ancient, middle-aged—it was all the same to us then.) Forty used to be the age of grown-ups. Now it seems more like the beginning of pretending not to be a grown-up, though it can be hard to believe this as you negotiate with a six-year-old about how many bites of pasta he has to eat before dessert.

Forty is also the age of stuff. For those of us who once wanted to backpack across Europe, this can be hard to accept, but nonetheless, forty-year-olds need dozens of shoes, state-of-the-art exercise equipment, the latest skin-care products, and most of all, closet space. They also need a book about how to turn forty.

One more thing: enjoy forty because once you turn fifty, you'll wish you could do it all over again.

You can remember thinking your parents were really, really old when they were younger than you are now.

Golf is starting to seem sort of cool.

Getting pregnant without medical intervention seems terribly quaint.

You don't *care* about mileage or pollution. You just want the damn SUV, okay?

A friend calls to invite you to lunch, and you reply, "How does November 12 two years from now sound?"

You haven't added to your thong collection in quite a while.

You could be the hippest person on the planet,
but no college kid would ever
think of you as a peer.

It really *is* too late to change your mind and go to veterinary school.

Your handwriting may still be legible to someone, but that someone is no longer you.

In two years, you've never stumbled upon an episode of *Seinfeld* that you haven't seen already.

You'd just as soon have cereal for dinner.

Suddenly, you are overcome by the urge to come up with a new "look" for yourself . . . but you can't be bothered.

It's not that the romance is gone, but you've definitely reached the "his and her bathrooms" stage of life.

A kid you once babysat is now your lawyer.

Watching *Mystery Science Theater 3000* sounds
so much more enticing than a night on the town.

You wonder if you can put off organizing your files for
long enough that you'll die and someone else will have
to do it.

You got all the way to work without noticing that you
were wearing one loafer and one clog.

At your checkups, the doctor has begun to ask if you're
sexually active.

Your college-alumni committee seems to think
you should be able to make a zillion-dollar
donation.

Suddenly you can see like an eighteen-year-old! Thank you, LASIK.

Someone offers you a seat on the bus. And you don't refuse.

You no longer look around, startled, when someone calls you Mommy.

Your kids are now more embarrassed by you than you are by your parents.

That 70s Show has started hitting the 80s.

You finally admit that you hate noisy restaurants and loud parties.

You carry a tube of lip balm
in every pocket.

You talk three hours a day about
how you get five hours of
sleep a night.

E now stands for "epidural."

You'd rather skip vacation than go camping—even at one of those campgrounds with running water at each site.

You can't hand the phone to someone else when telephone pollsters call and ask to speak to the head of the household.

When you go to a movie you invariably comment, "You know, theaters make all their profits at the concession stand."

Your son's math homework is too hard for you.

The years have seriously battered your sense of ironic detachment.

You wonder why Lands' End can't sell
more bathing suits with skirts.

You get professionally made up before having your passport photo taken.

Comb-overs are starting to make a certain kind of sense.

You know way too much about driveway sealants.

You've started to suspect that kids today have it a lot easier than they did when you were a kid.

You're not sure if it's still called "weed" anymore.

You expect your breakfast cereal to cure you, not entertain you.

What Pass for Thrills at Forty

○ Finding a shortcut.

○ Paper towels with a paisley border.

○ Heated car seats.

○ Buying 2% milk instead of 1%.

○ Telling the hairdresser you want bangs.

○ Seeing a girl you went to high school with in a bit part on *Law & Order*.

○ The clogged toilet that fixed itself.

○ The babysitter admires your Burberry.

○ A new Swiffer WetJet.

○ Cheesecake-flavored yogurt.

- Your new automatic eyeglass cleaner.

- Reorganizing your closet.

- Little white lies in your Christmas letter.

- Really hot Indian food.

- A subscription to *People*.

- Raising your pulse to 180 after doing the stationary bike for five minutes.

- Knitting a sweater.

- Collecting five gallons of pennies.

- Rearranging the furniture in the den.

- Getting the car washed.

You're pinning all your hopes

on sunscreen.

The sound of a leaf blower in your neighbor's yard drives you mad.

There's no longer a chance that when religious recruiters come to your door, they'll ask, "Are your parents at home?"

You are now expected to spend half your day on the slopes helping a preschooler learn how to snowplow.

You realize that your life's dream could be blighted by a building inspector.

Crying no longer gets you anywhere.

Each week you recognize fewer and fewer names in the "Weddings" section.

It seems as though you spend the better part of each weekend lacing up Peewee hockey skates . . .

. . . that is, if you're not driving to soccer games in the next state.

You give away your Hush Puppies loafers, realizing that they now look grandparent-y instead of cool.

You're no longer afraid that you'll pull the lever the wrong way when you vote.

You can't wait for your first colonoscopy—the drugs are supposed to be so great.

The Quiet Car on Amtrak = heaven.

You still feel like a kid, but your
friends are turning into
your parents.

You would like to slap the entire cast of *Friends*.

You have your own secretary.

You're a secretary for an MBA who's fifteen years younger than you.

People in their thirties expect you to pick up the check.

The Jell-O shots at your tailgate party are made with sugar-free Jell-O.

You pat yourself on the back for (generally) being too young to die of natural causes.

Your childhood collection of Breyer model horses would fetch a pretty penny on eBay.

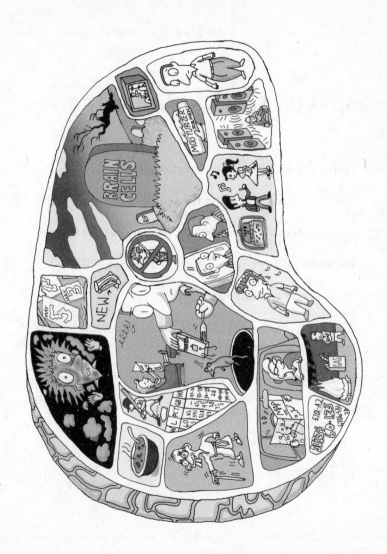

Inside the Forty-year-old Male Brain

○ Is this old-man nose hair or just regular?

○ Do pleated pants disguise the problem or magnify it?

○ Vehicle identification numbers of every car I've owned.

○ I'm definitely too old to be drafted even in WWIII.

○ Theme song to *Happy Days*.

○ People wouldn't have to do so much laundry if they bought new socks every week.

○ Is our anniversary this week or next?

○ Primetime TV schedules 1972–1987.

○ That ole standby recipe for chili.

○ Baseball statistics.

- Is wet-hair gel over?

- Moisturizer for men? Really?!

- Bose Accoustimass 10 Series III vs. Bose Accoustimass 6 Series II vs. Bose Accoustimass 5 Series IV vs. Bose Accoustimass 10 Series II vs. Sony.

- Brain cells killed by booze consumed the weekend Danny's parents went to Cape Cod.

- If you dissolve Styrofoam in gasoline and set it on fire, you get a blaze that will pretty much burn forever.

- Is Jerry Lewis still alive?

- It's not fair that I have to empty the mousetraps every time.

- Would it kill her to learn to read a map?

- The time we had the car-to-car fireworks war driving home from high school, and Ralph threw the cherry bomb into Duncan's car.

You've finally finished paying off your own student loans—just in time for your kids to start private school.

Your tasteful engagement ring is starting to look cheap.

Your son asks if you would please walk twenty feet behind him at the mall.

You develop more than a passing interest in what's going to happen to Social Security.

You've reached the point where your kids are too old to fool by spelling out the word b-a-b-y-s-i-t-t-e-r.

You actually hear yourself say, "They call that music?!"

You take consolation from the fact that you still qualify for the short-incision or "Boomer" face-lift.

Construction workers no longer look up from their lunches when you walk by.

You can't fantasize about marrying into the Royal Family—all the good ones are taken.

You always carry a pack of Kleenex somewhere on your person.

You're getting wrinkles and breaking out simultaneously.

You've lost your illusions about what wheatgrass can do for you.

People wince and avert their eyes

as you stride onto the

nude beach.

You tell yourself that a stroll through the park can pass for exercise.

Stretch fabrics are your secret best friend.

You'd never dream of sleeping on the floor or even on someone's couch.

You'd rather stay up all night than leave the dishes from tonight's dinner party on the kitchen counter until tomorrow morning.

You put off your dreams of "financial freedom" until age fifty.

Even though you gave your first child only organic, hand-prepared baby food, you let your second child eat sugar cubes for breakfast.

You hire a lighting consultant
when you redecorate.

You've lost interest in the travails of Mike and Elizabeth in *For Better or For Worse.*

A girl you knew in high school is a grandmother.

You can't get away with collecting comic books anymore.

There's a jar of silver polish in your cupboard.

You automatically say "No, thanks" when the waiter asks if you want to see the dessert menu.

You wouldn't dream of just hopping on a bike. Now it's got to be on a titanium-framed mountain bike, in biking shorts and a fancy helmet.

You have to control your swearing because of the kids.

You lose your car keys, then lose them again three minutes later.

You're beginning to think that learning bridge might be a good idea.

You used to dread the thought of selling out. Now you long for the chance.

You no longer expect holidays to be fun.

You wonder if maybe it's time to buy a tuxedo instead of renting one every time.

The under-thirty-fives on your softball team are starting to lose patience with you.

There's no chance that anyone will mistake you for a trophy wife.

Inside the Forty-year-old Female Brain

○ Do I need collagen or do I just smile too much?

○ If that's a chin hair, I'm killing myself right now.

○ If I do Amy's carpool next Thursday and Wendy does Meg's carpool Friday and Rachel does my carpool on . . .

○ Why did I buy a new "Verve" when I have two unopened tubes at home and, besides, it's the same color as Chanel #39, which I have three of, but what if they discontinue "Verve"? I'd better buy more "Verve."

○ I can't be this fat. The dry cleaners must have shrunk my pants.

○ Damn! I forgot to call Mark back!

○ Should I go to the bank, then the post office, then lunch or the bank, then lunch, and then—or should I skip lunch and go to Pilates or what if I go to Pilates and then . . . ?

○ Brain tumor! . . . No, just a crease from my baseball cap.

○ What should I wear to Diane's wedding eight months from now?

○ She must have had Botox.

○ Make eyebrow appointment; do taxes; buy cantaloupe; learn French; leave Ted.

○ Location of every public bathroom in the city.

○ Lyrics to every Camp Pinecliffe song.

○ Sarah Jessica & Matthew's baby = James.

○ "Who" or "whom"?

○ Maggie owes me $144.62.

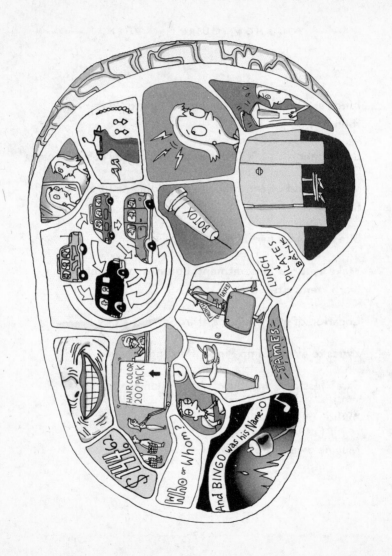

Your six-year-old set up the DVD player for you.

You get to see firsthand that the chaperones have an even worse time at middle-school dances than the kids.

You start slurring on your second glass of wine.

Hiking has totally lost its appeal.

You've learned that a relationship can have a "rocky patch" that's five years long.

No one tells you to sit up straight.

Your niece screams with laughter when she sees what Barbies looked like when you were little.

The bartender cards everyone
in your group but you.

You suddenly think, "How rude that nobody bothers to RSVP!"

You can't see the point of opening the mail anymore—it's only bills.

There's no reason to listen to your answering machine either—it's just your mom wondering why you haven't called.

You and the guys spend Friday night at a chainsaw demo at the lumber store.

You find yourself giving anti-smoking lectures . . .

. . . and anti-drinking sermons . . .

. . . and pro-yoga rants.

Midnight seems
awfully late.

You worry about your cholesterol, even though you're not sure which is the good kind and which is the bad.

You try to convince yourself that it's a freckle, not a liver spot.

You actually say that someone is too thin!

Costume parties don't seem like crazy fun anymore. More like self-conscious juvenilia.

You quit the twenty-mile walkathon after eleven miles.

You decide to play it safe and enroll the kids in religious education class.

At Least When You're Forty You Don't Have to Worry About . . .

○ Making toasts at your friends' twenty-first birthdays.

○ Making toasts at your friends' (first) weddings.

○ Your first job interview.

○ The Big Three-Oh.

○ Losing your fake I.D.

○ Losing your virginity.

○ Finding your first gray hair. (You already found it long ago.)

○ Participating in a poetry slam.

○ What to major in.

○ Whether you should still try to enter a few beauty pageants.

○ Whether you have a chance to make the Olympics.

○ Fraternity hazings.

○ Winning a wet T-shirt contest.

○ Someone finding your beer bongs.

You know more about the
Teletubbies than you do
about the President.

You get to catch up with all your friends at the electrologist's office.

You iron your own shirts instead of waiting for your mom to do them when she visits.

You fuss if a single drop of red wine gets onto the tablecloth.

You know all your credit card numbers by heart.

You serve an assortment of salty, bitter, wrinkled olives when friends come over—and your friends like them!

The ads on your favorite television shows are all for detergent and vitamins.

You could read the menu if only
your arms would grow
one inch longer.

You're *this* close to putting "guest soaps" in the bathroom.

You own sixteen handbags.

You own four wristwatches—and to think that once upon a time you couldn't be bothered to know what time it was!

You rationalize that candy bar by telling yourself that the peanuts have lots of fiber.

You give up sleeping in the nude because it wouldn't be good for the children.

You haven't cannonballed into a
swimming pool in years.

Your parents are starting to offload all their old junk onto you—stuff that has so much sentimental value that they want *you* to throw it out instead of them.

You have to stop and consider whether going sledding is worth the trouble.

You get into a fender bender, and there are no grown-ups you can beg to make it all go away.

You have fancy "gift" paperclips instead of plain office-supply ones.

It's been months since you last spoke to your siblings, let alone saw them.

Your idea of a vacation would be
for everyone else to go away
for a couple of days.

Your remarkable spelling skills have dissapeered.

Getting lost in a car is no longer a romantic adventure.

You're more interested in selling your old stuff on eBay than in buying new stuff.

You couldn't live without the redial button.

You and your cellulite have come to terms.

Your idea of a younger man is the age your father was when you were born.

You can't find time to read the newspaper. You get your news by "intuition."

You've developed a glandular need
to own real estate.

You realize that if the house were on fire, the first thing you'd grab would be your under-eye concealer.

You are one of a dying breed who remember what Smurfs were.

Belts have been phased out of your wardrobe.

You seriously wonder if cruises are so horrible after all.

You don't know anyone who's single.

You receive two phone calls in one week from people who want to sell you life insurance.

At the Pinkers' Dinner Party

○ Most guests brought hostess presents.

○ The Redlers were late because their babysitter was late.

○ There was a scented candle in the bathroom.

○ The Pinkers' preschooler had drawn the place cards.

○ There was one single man and one single woman, and we were all dying to know what they thought of each other.

○ Everyone admired the new antique breakfront in the living room.

○ Lucy made horseradish from scratch.

○ A salad course was served.

○ Meghan could not eat the tomatoes because she had developed an allergy to them.

○ The big topic was Richard's sperm motility.

○ After dinner, the men talked about football in the living room and the women talked about hair color in the kitchen.

○ Stuart got plastered and we talked about it for days.

○ The Redlers left early because Mike had to make a five a.m. flight to Cincinnati the next day.

○ The evening was over by ten.

○ The Fowlkeses' Lexus was blocking your Expedition in the driveway.

○ Two couples sent thank-you flowers the next day; two couples sent handwritten thank-you notes; and the rest emailed.

An awful lot of new Sesame Street characters
seem to have sneaked onto the show
without your noticing.

You find yourself starting a lot of sentences with "Life is too short to . . ."

You have a cookbook full of recipes in your head. And no time to make any of them.

You've gotten used to what you look like in mirrors. (Except for three-way mirrors in fitting rooms—a never-ending source of shock and horror.)

You have lower back pain.

You can't help but correct the grammar of others.

You actually pay attention to your electric bill.

Your best friend teaches you
how to wear a scarf.

Instead of searching for pornography online, you find sites that will calculate your body mass index.

You decide Mexican food's not worth the heartburn.

Putting on a miniskirt makes you feel as if you're wearing a costume.

Consumer Reports has become your favorite magazine.

You go to a lot of trouble to put in a fancy bird feeder, but then can't be bothered to fill it.

You can't visit your parents' house without casting a covetous eye over certain pieces of furniture.

You haven't done anything special for New Year's Eve in ten years.

You have a nice umbrella. (And you haven't left it in a restaurant so far.)

Putting coins into the parking meter has lost its thrill.

You can't believe you had that goatee a few years ago.

You've started using *exactly* the expressions your mom used when you were a child—like "If you can't say something nice, don't say anything at all."

The time has come to add a couple of houseplants.

Even if you got one of those insanely
big tennis rackets, your game
would not improve.

"Please take me off your call list" is as close to phone sex as you get these days.

You realize that from now on, every birthday will be an embarrassment.

You feel as if the bad things happening to the environment are your fault.

You routinely withdraw sums at the ATM that would have terrified you in your twenties.

The first snowfall of the year has lost its winter-wonderland charm—all you can see are hours of shoveling.

You wouldn't mind sitting down
at cocktail parties.

Words to Live By
(for the Limited Time You've Got Left)

○ "The lovely thing about being forty is that you can appreciate twenty-five-year-old men more."
—Colleen McCullough

○ "At the age of twenty, we don't care what the world thinks of us; at thirty, we worry about what it thinks of us; at forty, we discover that it wasn't thinking of us at all." —Anonymous

○ "The first forty years of life give us the text; the next thirty supply the commentary."
—Arthur Schopenhauer

○ "Women deserve to have more than twelve years between the ages of twenty-eight and forty."
—James Thurber

○ "When I passed forty I dropped pretense, 'cause men like women who got some sense." —Maya Angelou

○ "At twenty years of age the will reigns; at thirty the wit; at forty the judgment." —Benjamin Franklin

○ "At thirty, man suspects himself a fool; knows it at forty, and reforms his plan." —Edward Young

○ "I'm not forty; I'm eighteen with twenty-two years' experience." —Anonymous

○ "Every man over forty is a scoundrel."
—George Bernard Shaw

○ "Life begins at forty—but so do fallen arches, rheumatism, faulty eyesight, and the tendency to tell a story to the same person, three or four times."
—William Feather

○ "Forty is the old age of youth, fifty is the youth of old age." —Victor Hugo

○ "Be wise with speed; a fool at forty is a fool indeed."
—Edward Young

You meet up with your friends and the first ten minutes are spent reassuring each other. ("You look good!" "No, you look good!" "No, *you* do!")

Your house is full of at least 120 years' worth of clutter.

You're too stressed to have a midlife crisis.

You get in a car accident and think that you'd better not get taken to the hospital today, because you're wearing your husband's old boxers with a black lace push-up bra.

You just spent more on a vacuum cleaner than your parents did on the down payment for their first house.

Your husband gives you a bread machine
for your anniversary . . .

. . . and your wife gives you a fat-measuring bathroom scale for your birthday.

You spend more than a week discussing what camp your children should go to.

You're too much of a wuss to give other highway drivers the finger anymore.

Matthew Perry once seemed the same age as you in a good way. Now he seems the same age as you in a bad way.

All those designer clothes you once looked so cool in are only fit for the costume box at the nursery school.

You shave your legs only for
special occasions, like
New Year's Eve.

You subscribe to *More*.

You just about die of joy when your twelve-year-old burns one of your CDs.

You smile knowingly when twentysomethings vow that their childbirth experience will be completely natural.

You can deal with the fact that you'll never get your partner to lose weight.

You're starting to think you *deserve* a diamond tennis bracelet.

You're pretty sure your eyelashes were thicker last time you checked.

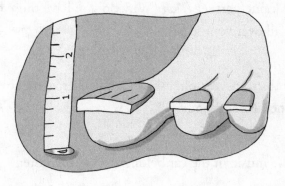

You're also pretty sure your toenails were thinner last time you checked.

You're starting to think you *deserve* a Porsche.

Your kindergartner asks, "Why do you have those blue lines all over your legs?"

Your thirteen-year-old asks, "Can you drive me to Planned Parenthood?"

All the music in the car belongs to your children.

Going bowling with your pals used to seem edgy, but now you worry that you're one of those people in a bowling league.

Tears come to your eyes as you fly over the Grand Canyon.

You either switch to margarine for your health—or switch from margarine back to butter because at this point, there's no point in caring about your health anymore.

You visit Paris and realize you have forgotten every last French word you learned in college.

Someone you know is on the cover of *Newsweek* . . . for white-collar crime.

You now understand that the only person who will walk the dog is you.

You've given up snapping photos of every little cute thing your kids do . . . which is just as well, since you'll never get around to putting all those photos into albums.

Even your young friends are getting old.

Your parents no longer knock themselves out choosing your birthday presents.

It is highly likely that Polly, your African Grey parrot, will outlive you.

You just gave your eight-year-old a lecture on the perils of a bad credit rating.

You will never live long enough to read all of the unread books in your bookcase . . .

Your friends are taking up weird hobbies
like weaving and parasailing.

Ditto the TiVo'd television shows . . .

In fact, you won't even live long enough to catch up on your back issues of *People*.

You weigh more now than you did five years ago when you weren't on a diet.

You can't remember why you're so happy, and then it dawns on you: you just had the windows in your house washed.

You don't even have to look at the labels—you've memorized the nutritional values.

You're counting on lasers to fix everything that's wrong with you in the future.

It would probably be over the top if
you got your eyebrow pierced.

You decide gardening's not so bad.

You've finally stopped sending away for graduate-school catalogs.

All the movie stars are so young these days that you might as well be watching kids play dress-up.

You realize, with a sickening sense of dread, that what your teachers always told you was true: nobody achieves success without hard work.

No one needs to tell you that you'll never break the five-minute mile.

You've finally abandoned your plans to hitchhike cross-country with your college roommates.

Things You'll Never Say Again

○ "I hope to dance with the New York City Ballet Company someday."

○ "Do you have this bikini in a smaller size?"

○ "So I was in the mosh pit and . . ."

○ "I can't wait for my birthday!"

○ "This new diet will solve all my problems."

○ "Me? I'm going to take the year off."

○ "No complaints so far."

○ "I'm going to bake on the beach all week."

○ "Let's drive all night so we can do the trip without stopping."

- "They'll take care of me—that's what parents are for."

- "Watch me do a full split!"

- "So what if it's late? I can sleep as late as I want tomorrow."

- "It's a problem. No matter what I eat, I can't seem to put on weight."

- "I need a good, long book. Any recommendations?"

- "I think I'll start smoking cigarettes. It's so cool!"

- "I saw them on *After Hours*."

- "Gosh, time goes by sooooooooooooo slowly."

- "Sex twice in one night? Sure!"

- "Who needs health insurance?"

You can't remember the plots of 90 percent of the books you've read . . .

. . . and the other 10 percent you can't remember reading.

You have mastered the art of pretending to hear what someone is saying at a big party.

You have mastered the art of making one drink last for four hours.

Somehow, a minivan has ended up in your garage.

Somehow, a Little Tykes minivan has ended up in your living room.

While you're folding laundry, you're struck
by how huuuuuuuuuge your underpants
have become over the years.

You turn to the obituaries before reading anything else in the paper.

You wish you had paid attention when your mom was teaching you basic sewing skills.

You wish you had paid attention when your dad was teaching you basic budgeting skills.

Some of the stuff on network TV shocks even you.

You can't believe Burma is Myanmar now.

There's a ton of nice monogrammed stationery in your desk.

You've been using a calculator so long that you no longer remember even the "twos" in the multiplication tables.

It seems more and more unlikely that you and Cameron Diaz will get together.

You flat-out bawl watching that TV commercial where the little girl calls her grandmother to say "I love you."

Your gynecologist asks you whether you've ever considered adopting.

VH1 is starting to seem more worthwhile than MTV.

The woman who cuts your hair tells you that you don't need *too* much "product."

You wish there were a snooze alarm on your biological clock.

You refuse to assemble another toy on Christmas Eve.

You finally realize that you'll never get that novel published.

Newspapers keep running articles about how your generation is destroying the economy.

All the bridesmaids from your wedding are now divorced.

You think, "Oh, age doesn't mean anything, it's how you feel . . . Oh, how you feel doesn't mean anything, it's how you look . . . Oh, how you look doesn't mean anything, it's your attitude . . . Oh, your attitude doesn't mean anything, it's what drugs you have at your disposal."

Things You Used to Buy vs. Things You Buy Now

Six-pack of Rolling Rock.	Six cases of Juicy Juice.
Smashing Pumpkins CD.	Actual pumpkin for Halloween.
Patchouli oil.	Deodorant.
$200 basketball shoes.	Knee brace.
Size 6.	Size 12.
Standby third-class railway ticket to Nepal.	Premium cable subscription, including the Travel Channel.

Army surplus store backpack.	Totebag received for giving $100 to public radio during pledge drive.
Henna.	Nice 'n Easy.
Big Mac.	Grilled McChicken.
Diamond embedded in front tooth.	Adult braces.
Swatch.	Citizen.
Frappucino.	No-fat Chai Latte.
Pot.	Potting soil.
Scalped tickets to U2 concert.	Discount tickets to car wash.

You have a deep new respect for
your rotator cuff.

You've become cynical about things you once held dear (like the films of John Hughes).

You round up all the clothes you thought you'd fit back into one day, and drop them off at Goodwill.

A girl in your daughter's eighth-grade class just got signed by a modeling agency.

The only Top Ten song that you've heard is the R&B ballad.

The only growth spurt you can look forward to is sideways.

You wonder if maybe it's time
to switch to decaf.

The cutest, meanest girl you knew in college is
still cute and mean—and now, really successful as
well.

It's not your imagination. You *are* getting more
forgetful.

All the birthday-party invitations you receive say "No
gifts."

You have begun *The Education of Henry
Adams* eight times without getting beyond
page ten.

It's likely that the last five gadgets you bought will not
be used more than once.

Facts to Face at Forty

○ The body you have now is the body you'll have for the rest of your life, except that it will get worse.

○ Nothing works on stretch marks.

○ If you were to dump your partner and reconnect with your high-school sweetheart, it wouldn't work out.

○ If you were to dump your job and try to make it as a ski instructor, it also wouldn't work out.

○ No rock stars will ever ask you to be the drummer in their band—or even to sing backup.

○ You're not going to find that golf club you lost six years ago.

○ Expensive skin-care products won't turn the clock back any better than cheap ones.

○ Most household hints don't work. The ones that do, you'll forget.

○ Chocolate ice cream stains are permanent.

○ Your spouse does not have a secret fortune he/she was waiting to tell you about when you'd proved your loyalty.

It's been a long time since anyone
called you a wunderkind.

People may still think of you as cool, but in their minds they add "for a forty-year-old."

For the first time in your life, you say "That's neither here nor there" during an argument.

A kid you bump into on the sidewalk says, "Excuse me, sir."

You've been asking an awful lot of your Hip Slip lately.

Your graduating class's reports in the alumni magazine have migrated backward toward the middle of the section.

The Victoria's Secret catalog makes
your heart sink.

You pray that downloading music files won't get any more complicated.

You astonish your parents by taking them out for a lovely dinner at an expensive restaurant. Without even wanting to break bad news to them or anything!

You sign up for ballroom dancing lessons.

You figure you might as well let that *GQ* subscription go.

You can actually gather up handfuls of your stomach.

You're pretty sure that if your current relationship ended, you'd choose celibacy over having anyone new see you naked.

You buy paper towels in bulk at Costco.

You have a broad assortment of "trouser socks."

You are now coaching T-ball, the world's most boring sport.

It's getting *so* hard to put on eyeliner in the mirror!

To your astonishment, you're sort of turning into a Republican.

Suddenly you're one of the idiots trying to get too much luggage into the overhead storage compartment.

Only if you lose seventy-five pounds, get a full body lift, and hire a personal shopper will you be ready for your high-school reunion.

Things You Never, Ever, Ever, Ever, Ever Thought You'd Find Yourself Doing

- Wearing "comfort-waist" jeans.

- Saying "Hey, keep it down!" to some kids at the movies.

- Being afraid of teenagers lounging outside a store.

- Checking the nutrition label for trans fats.

- Reading the "Week in Review" section.

○ Buying a lollipop for a toddler in a shopping cart (your toddler and your cart) to make her quiet down.

○ Having your back waxed.

○ Sucking up to real grown-ups to get into the Field Club.

○ Yelling at other members of your household to turn off the lights when they leave a room.

○ Joining a book group.

○ Watching *Good Morning America* (and going to bed before *Late Night* is on).

○ Going to a chiropractor.

You have opinions about the
best way to make gravy.

In a fit of self-improvement, you buy some Teaching Company tapes about the history of philosophy. (They will sit unopened in your car for the next twenty years.)

None of your birthday cakes have candles anymore.

You're not sure whether what you have is "knee trouble" or just a sore knee.

You're the one who has to put the roof rack on the car before vacations.

"Health and wellness" catalogs have started coming in the mail.

Finding the perfect moisturizer
is more important to you
than finding God.

You hear yourself making a rule
about no Play-Doh in the
living room.

Naps seem a lot more important than they used to.

You spend an entire Saturday using the floor sander you rented from the hardware store.

You realize that you're the one who has to explain about Santa Claus.

You now understand why your parents did some of the things they did.

You make your first appointment with the podiatrist.

You can't get babysitters to call you by your first name.

Real-estate ads have become
your pornography.

You wonder if maybe, just maybe,
you look like an idiot when
you dance.

You realize it's time to stop thinking of politicians your age as "adults" and start thinking of them as peers.

You've started to notice that all the twentysomethings in sitcoms have apartments you couldn't possibly afford.

You brag about your daughter's home run in softball.

You've started to consider snowboarders a menace.

Both of your cars are in the shop.

Welcome to a Forty-Year-Old's Medicine Cabinet!

○ Lubricant drops for dry eyes.

○ Four kinds of tweezers.

○ Vaniqa.

○ Facial-hair bleach.

○ Sugar wax hair remover kit (doesn't work).

○ Home electrolysis kit (doesn't work).

○ Anti-snore nose squeezer (doesn't work).

○ Earplugs (see above).

○ Chanel No. 5—Christmas present from parents, never used because it smells too "elderly."

○ Gas-X.

○ Water Pik dentist persuaded you to buy, used once and forgotten.

○ Ultra-magnifying mirror worthy of horror chamber.

○ Seven brands of hand cream.

○ Nine brands of sunscreen.

○ "Men's" vitamins for "potency."

○ Parsley capsules for bad breath.

○ Shampoo for tinted hair.

You have to ask your children to explain what's so funny about that joke on the Video Music Awards.

You're *pretty* sure you're not old enough to need a rubber mat in the tub—but you decide you'd better get one just in case.

You're secretly glad about all those laws banning smoking in public.

You wonder if it's really necessary for boxers to hit each other that hard.

You've turned into one of those people who write letters of complaint to the phone company and your congressman.

You shout "Down in front!" at the

Bruce Springsteen concert . . .

. . . and vow that next time you're sitting on the mezzanine instead of standing on the floor.

You wouldn't dream of buying fireworks even if they were legal in your state.

You think nothing of spending thirty dollars on a bottle of wine.

You'd like to go to the demonstration, but it's supposed to rain.

You put the cat on a low-calorie diet.

Getting out of a chair causes you to make a small, involuntary sound of protest.

The mention of Viagra doesn't
get such a big guffaw out
of you any longer.

You've either mastered parallel parking or given up on it.

Same with making piecrust.

The clothes at the Gap look a little too youthful this season.

You buy books like this one.

You admit to thirty-five.

You're about to turn fifty.

ABOUT THE AUTHORS

ANN HODGMAN is the author of forty-five children's books and three cookbooks. With Patty Marx and Lisa Birnbach, she has coauthored the *1,003 Great Things About . . .* series. She lives in Washington, Connecticut, with her husband, their two children, and many, many pets.

PATRICIA MARX was the first woman to write for the *Harvard Lampoon* and has since published in *The New Yorker, Atlantic, The New York Times, Vogue,* and *Spy.* She was a staff writer for *Saturday Night Live* and *Rugrats,* and has written for many other TV shows. She has also written several screenplays and a number of books, including *How to Regain Your Virginity* and *Now Everybody Really Hates Me.* She teaches comedy writing at New York University.